Disorientation and the Weather

poems by

Dorinda Hale

Finishing Line Press
Georgetown, Kentucky

Disorientation and the Weather

Copyright © 2018 by Dorinda Hale
ISBN 978-1-63534-434-9 First Edition
All rights reserved under International and Pan-American Copyright Conventions. No part of this book may be reproduced in any manner whatsoever without written permission from the publisher, except in the case of brief quotations embodied in critical articles and reviews.

ACKNOWLEDGMENTS

Grateful acknowledgment to the editors of publications in which these poems first appeared, some in earlier versions:

Appalachia: "Sleeping by the Pacific: Guatemala"
Aspect: "Disorientation and the Weather"
Atlanta Review: "License to Fly," "Christmas Card"
Bellingham Review: "Chichicastenango"
Cream City Review: "Modified Rapture," "A New Year in Vermont"
Embers: "Consort"
North Shore Magazine: "10 ° F. December 20"
Passager: "After Grief"
Soundings East: "The Museum Guard"
Wilderness House Literary Review: "Companion Piece," "Rationale," and "Choosing a Site for a Lean-To"

Publisher: Leah Maines
Editor: Christen Kincaid
Cover Art: Parrish Dobson
Author Photo: Susan Wilson
Cover Design: Elizabeth Maines McCleavy

Printed in the USA on acid-free paper.
Order online: www.finishinglinepress.com
    also available on amazon.com

Author inquiries and mail orders:
Finishing Line Press
P. O. Box 1626
Georgetown, Kentucky 40324
U. S. A.

Table of Contents

License to Fly 1

Consort 3

Companion Piece 5

Rationale 6

Christmas Card 7

10° F. December 20 8

Disorientation and the Weather 9

Sleeping by the Pacific: Guatemala 10

Chichicastenango 11

The Museum Guard 12

The Begotten 13

Transference 14

By Any Other Name 15

Modified Rapture 16

Choosing a Site for a Lean-To 17

A New Year in Vermont 18

Fourth of July 20

After Grief 22

For my mother, Miriam Munson Hale (1912-2003),
who wanted to say these things

LICENSE TO FLY

In a night sky over the Atlantic—
past Gander past Bangor—
just short of home
comes your longed-for call:
"Is there anyone aboard who can fly this plane?"
You can, of course.

You stride to the cockpit.
Passengers wild with hope
whisper, "It's a woman."
From the captain's seat
console lights
a familiar galaxy,
each star and constellation
burning in its own color.
Your slightest touch moves all—
what are rudder and flaps
but extensions of you?

The pilots groan on the floor; they dream
of the wives and children you'll return to them.

The tower crackles, "What do you need?"
"Coordinates. Tell me where I am,
where you are—I'll be there."
You know all the angles,
it's only a matter of feeling the wind
the ancient, prevailing wind.

You begin the descent.
The sadness of landing encroaches,
the tower of voices speaks more insistently:
 "Who are you? How did you know?"
Your perfect approach makes them think
there might not be disaster.
They decide they believe in God.

Touchdown.
The passengers will mob you
and cry, won't understand—
they think you did it for them.

CONSORT

There is no sound but a flute
stabbing air in the distance.
If I say
the song is the faint, brilliant dirge
of a fife still piping to a lost war,
you might sense its melancholy
but not its lushness:
orange wind in a field of poppies.

Implied by the sound
are moving fingers
and enough warm breath
to make a silver tube sweat.
I know this
because I've seen a swab
go through an instrument
and come out wet.

All this concern for the instrument, and look!
the flutist has swallowed the flute.
This is not funny.
Because the song goes on.
It must be established
who is playing.

Is it you?

For years I heard you perform
in famous concert halls
for large, adoring audiences.
I myself practiced often,
learned how to cadenza magnificently,

and became a virtuoso section
for the soloist,
who often seemed to be you,
though it could have been construed to be me
by virtue of my position
on the stage.

It must be established
who is playing.

COMPANION PIECE

He looks at her boxer's crouch,
the report from her eyes of a gift,
and feels them as wooden rumors
with designs upon the truth.
But there she goes dead ahead into speaking
nevertheless, of his hands, how they gnarl
around secrets in his knees.
Of her hands as they spot pearly
the exact place on the page
where something laughs and leaves the room.

RATIONALE

Because of the way you feed, needing flagons for cups
and spoons big as amphitheaters, I can't set your table.

With a throat for sucking juice from mangoes
a singer hosannas above the chorus. The sound fastens me.

As you loosen, how is it possible for me to ratify
your toppling wordstack and respond to all your rests?

CHRISTMAS CARD

Backed up against winter woods that are not lovely, dear
though certainly dark and deep
a small red house
simply gabled, without windows
a child's drawing with the requisite twist of smoke.
Somebody's home,
fire inside
the only invitation.

How calming the firm edge between snowfield and woods
where treetops limn a cobalt night sky
with a fringe of bruised lace.
A single star, round in its bigness,
could pass for the moon, can't account for
stippled and cross-hatched snow—
shadow requires light.

I send you this on the darkest day of the year,
a day without which light's only a burden,
to tell you I live in this house with you,
held there by bounty in isolated beauty.

10° F. DECEMBER 20

Sidewalk dogs peer
through bottom panes,
their people drinking
coffee, buying cakes.
That one has turned
tail and flopped; this
one remains, sifting
a delta of warm smells
for the familiar.
All over town, tinsel
glances off their sighs.

DISORIENTATION AND THE WEATHER

Looking for proof that our symmetry's right,
I recite your bedroom's unfamiliar geometry:
count five sides around the ceiling,
count limbs—eight in this bed—
and faces—two,
would count stairs or sheep
if I could then view calmly
the rest of us
and the doorjamb swollen open in August heat.
Outside, the streetcars whine about the summer drought,
slide their sound by on a tangent.
The crickets are holding their breath.

In the dark, I try to remember where your dresser is,
if there's a chair.
"What color is your rug?"
"Red."
"What's outside the window?"
"Morning glories on a chain-link fence."

We touch, and the air steps back from the window,
rain begins a soft windless fall,
grasses lap over in ease.
Rain in the nick of time.

SLEEPING BY THE PACIFIC: GUATEMALA

More than I can tell goes on here
where north is thinning into south:
the stars splay themselves
in unfamiliar ways.
If only I knew how to spell them out
for you in Boston.
Eighteen have shot north.

This is the first warm ocean
I've swum in. With each plunge
I hold back my skin,
expecting Cape Ann's cold gasp
remembering how it sprang us back
all nervy to the dunes.
Alone at dawn
I'll take the water's surprise again.

Now something edges up on me.
Six-foot breakers crumple
into disguise as watery amoebas,
sneak up the beach
undermine my sandy bed.

Deep beneath my back tectonic plates
grind toward another lurch.
Wait! What I know
and what I do not know
move against each other in the earth.

CHICHICASTENANGO

In a strange town sleeping dogs
make you think you deserve peace.
You've been here twenty minutes.

Just because you see Maya
on the church steps, do you
expect history to be yours?

to feel that your time is
important because you've read books?
These men burn Christian incense

to pagan gods. You read *Four Quartets*
at night in your pension,
purchase a candle to go on

when electricity fails.
Smoke. Words.
You can photograph both.

THE MUSEUM GUARD

Has a crush on the curator
which requires standing daily
in one room, or maybe three
guarding the absence of touch.

A mere overseer in the parish
of the eyes, he shifts legs
like a heron waiting for a fish,
wings precisely tucked.

THE BEGOTTEN

You won't become different
by dint of effort to repaint
the picture—

you'll always see the desired one
as hunger's tease
just beyond your grasp:

impervious to but not unhappy about
blandishment—satisfied to smile
or not smile.

You're consoled by old masters
who took centuries with Brunelleschi's
perspective, found footing in illusion—

though quickened
by their rebellious heirs'
fractured geometry and belief
in *passage*, a slither into space.

You like to think
the difference was only math,
the given remaining untouched—
that you can't change

because you were loved
at the riveting point
where two lines met:
this longing the gift bestowed.

TRANSFERENCE

I'm peevish and announce it: Peevish!
because I can't have you.

You laugh . . . a little . . . hmm . . .
the ambiguous all-purpose response.

Yet your eyes, inward-looking,
trip over something like rue.
Not unkindly, they flicker and sigh.

Unappeased, Hungry Ghosts move in
claim everything, in the clamor
each elbowing the other for precedence.
A veritable convention of desire.

I want to go back
to the not unkindly

soft yielding recognition
that held in the eyes' embrace
concocted tragedy.

BY ANY OTHER NAME

Fifty minutes, time to go.

We stop talking about the Sistine Chapel
how like the finger of God you are
or are not,
consider much was done
without touching.

Between us on the table
a vase of lavender roses,
escutcheons of enchantment
for the love-impaled—
stand-ins, some say,
for the imagined unattainable
blue rose.

Please take one that you like.

O happiness! Leave-taking eased.
A flower comes that I may go.

I choose a rose
balance its long spiny stem
awkwardly
in one hand—
thorns, a drop of water
where you drape
a white tissue (so many at hand!).

Carefully we wrap
against desiccation, wounding—
your fingers delicate and lovely
so deft, so . . . near
impossible imagined touch.

Not everything can be done
without.

MODIFIED RAPTURE

Circle a peak at timberline
        camisoled secretly in silk.
Keep trees to the left, crags to the right
        or reconnoiter at once, at once.

Walk downhill to daisies,
        browse and pluck.
Sweat but lightly, lightly
        (small damp curls at your neck).

Children, play loop-de-loo and hula hoop.
        Back in your dark room, see the flashlight
        beam a two-step on the wall.
Keep your pencils sharp.

Walk downhill to daisies.
Roll under the sea that swells above you.
Dot, dot your *i*'s.

CHOOSING A SITE FOR A LEAN-TO

Because the underbrush held "sign"
we knew that wild things
thrived in tangle, but the thicket
took our feet like mistakes,
and when roots held we jumped free
or fell.
If they tore from earth
we grunted, and jungled through.

Sometimes—hunched or crawling,
faces to the growth—we stalked
ourselves through a beard
of vegetation we couldn't name
to a clearing where blackberry bushes
disguised rotting logpiles
as walkways, and we'd suddenly
drop off shredded wood
into an airy twig-mash,
sham ground.

Sundown could make our return
a swagger in the dark:
we learned
by getting caught once
to enter the woods with time enough
to test our spot
to lie on the moss
and measure the tilt of response.

A NEW YEAR IN VERMONT
In memory of Mary Russell (1968-1974)

December 28
We liked your delirium better,
the magic convolutions of your cortex
pulling rabbits from the hat:
songs of arithmetic
jingles to friends and fetters.
It taxes our lexicon
to name your unreflective stillness.

> *Is she sleeping*
> *is she sleeping*
> *sister Mary*
> *sister Mary?*
> *Morning bells are ringing*
> *morning bells are ringing*
> . . . .
> . . . .

Bruises begin to ooze
where no instrument has probed
the seismology of tissue.
Doctors circle and date
in thick black ink
each new flood.

Oh my priests
what music do you hear
to circumscribe
this inner weeping of blood?

December 31
Yes doctors we agree that this brain formed from our coupling
should not persist since as you say it is no longer
the issue we can rightfully expect and yes we permit you
to attempt to wring some beauty from this death
since as you say the treatment has failed
although the disease has not recurred.
Yes we allow the machine's uncoupling
and the infinite lenitive needle
so that this riddle labeled body
bloated and pierced
this body sore beloved
may be stopped.

January 2
Our peace lies frozen and running
in the brook of this picture postcard
captioned, "Brilliant sun on snow
makes snug village sparkle."
A thin, tough membrane of anger
has settled over the hills.
Wearing long underwear and hiking boots
with city clothes for the trek to the grave
we could be a famous painting, still untitled.

FOURTH OF JULY

In the old boys' camp lodge, now your brother's house,
on the screened cathedral porch
with its cantilevered reach toward tall firs
that dress the steep bank to Wild Goose Pond—
summer conversation: bugs and weather.

Did you ever visit here?

Across the water, sounds of drink and laughter,
an empty bench high on the shore
looking back at us. Your old girlfriend
and her friend play "Stars and Stripes Forever"
on pipe and tabor, difficult breathy obbligato.

Did you want to marry her?

Suddenly a flood in the cabin next door: water
flows over sinks, squeezes through floorboards, drips off
siding. Three of us go after shovel and hoe,
dig out the septic tank. Wadded diapers
pop like dumplings from the outflow pipe.
The landlord, your brother, rages.

Did you love your brother?

Now a passionate debate about cooking:
Should we start a wood fire now? Or
perhaps use the grill? And mustn't
the chicken be pre-cooked? Will we die?
How long will this take, anyway?

Didn't you always enjoy a fine frenzy?

Josh, born on the Fourth, gone but a year,
for you we jammed a crosscut saw into a log
standing sentinel at the entrance,
neither a gate nor a signpost, barely a greeting.
Just a hint: a toothy pointing beyond the road
to old rock upthrust into a slash of sky,
the earth pierced but holding.

AFTER GRIEF

She remains in place, a site
and keeps her body with him
unbroken in a swell of light.

He's leaned away, though not in flight
hears a cadence meant for him
yet remains in place, a site

bold and burnished, hers despite
the keen constraint, the spell of rhythm.
Unbroken in a swell of light

our dead can sing to us, invite
a waning heart to shelter: an interim
that remains in place, a site

where porous love may dwell. What sleight
of hand unveiled this layered scrim
now unbroken in a swell of light

and let the soak of ties outright
claim her, hold him, allow them
to remain in place—a site
unbroken—in a swell of light?

Dorinda Hale, also published as Dori Hale, began writing poetry seriously while a graduate student at Western Washington University, where she earned an M.A. in English with a concentration in creative writing. During a long, eclectic career in a variety of positions—welfare caseworker, teacher, editor, housecleaner, typist, software documentation manager, translation project manager—she wrote and published sporadically in a number of journals. *Disorientation and the Weather* is her first chapbook. Most recently, her poems have appeared in *Atlanta Review, Wilderness House Literary Review,* and *Passager,* where "After Grief" was chosen for the 2017 poetry contest issue.

Dori Hale lives in Somerville, Massachusetts, and occasionally escapes to her primitive shack in Vermont, where she's pretty good with a chainsaw or brush hog.

www.ingramcontent.com/pod-product-compliance
Lightning Source LLC
LaVergne TN
LVHW041521070426
835507LV00012B/1744